THIS BOOK IS LOVINGLY DISTRIBUTED BY:

Lionheart Ministry

Roaring with His ferocious love, calling the church to repentance, restoration, and revival.

For more writing and to order online visit | www.lionheartministry.com

All content and rights are reserved and cannot be used without written consent.

Carrie is a daughter of the King, a sinner daily in need of His grace, running after His presence. She is blessed with a husband, Jonathan, a man of faithfulness and wisdom, her very best friend. Without him, these writings could not be birthed. His sacrifice and service to his family has made a way. Jonathan and Carrie are Co-founders of Lionheart Ministry, and are delighted to serve the Lord together through this way! Carrie is extravagantly blessed with two children. Her littles teach her daily of God's beauty, grace, and love. Her greatest joy is dancing with words of wonder and planting them onto pages with the Lord. Carrie's heart aims to serve God's people with His rich love, and she is praying and yearning for a revival to sweep over His church.

Carrie Christopher

A TREASURY OF HIS PROMISES,
POEMS, AND PROPHETIC POWER

Volume 1

A prayer for you

Praying each of these poems, scriptures and prophetic pieces will minister the very love of our Father in Heaven to your soul. Praying that freedom would come from them, as you intimately experience God as your creator, accessible through the sacrifice of His son Jesus Christ. Asking that the Holy Spirit's power would land on you with redemption, reformation and revival fire of glory.

I, Carrie Christopher, commit all of this book to the ultimate GLORY and dominion of Jesus Christ our Savior! All praises go to HIM who was, who is and who is to come. All scriptures are taken from the New International Version.

Special thanks to Rachel Dube and Lindsey Sullivan for generously lending their editing gifts to these words. Their encouragement and love are treasured. Special thanks to Lynne Hudson for partnering with me on a Holy Spirit mission, to minister to God's little ones with His Lavished love. Special thanks to Kayla Follin for designing and laying out these writings and drawings into a physical form.

For more writing and to order online visit lionheartministry.com

All content and rights are reserved and cannot be used without written consent.

Authored by: Carrie Christopher
Illustrated by: Lynne Hudson

His little ones are lavished by the love of the Father, always under His protection and saturated in the depth of His faithful promises, experiencing the living waters of the Word. The swirling butterflies represent the Holy Spirit as new life is breaking forth. As His little ones feel the tender love for God's creatures, they are experiencing the love of Jesus. The three hearts represent the Trinity, Royalty, Living Waters, & God's Glory.

- Lynne Hudson

About Illustrator Lynne Hudson

Lynne resides on the Gold Coast, Queensland, Australia and has been a professional artist for over forty years. You can find Lynne passionately teaching art classes and working on private commissions for clients, including illustrating Christian books and media. Experience Heaven's power coming down to earth, as she conducts prophetic and creative art workshops through her God-given giftings. God-inspired, and Holy Spirit saturated, Lynne has blessed many successful global art exhibitions with her works.

Lynne is an accomplished professional speaker, using her prophetic art and testimonies as a platform for His glory. The Lord has breathed into Lynne's words and art, an inspirational life story. Her testimony uniquely expresses her childhood love of painting, as the Lord carried her through a story of triumph over setbacks from the traditional art world. The Lord used these worldly setbacks to instead paint a new picture in her life, releasing many of her works through successful exhibitions in Australia and New York City.

Prophetic art changed Lynne's life forever, with the healing influence of Jesus Christ. The Lord radically healed her from the side effects of cancer, through prayer and experiencing a prophetic painting. From that time forward her life has been committed to the Lord to paint the poetic promises of His heart on a canvas of hope. Her journey marked a holy embracing of prophetic art — from live painting with worship, to private commissions and teaching courses on the magnitude of hearing from God through creativity.

Lynne's ability to hear from the Holy Spirit, and paint the courts of the heavenlies is lighting the church on fire with the radical love of Jesus Christ. Lynne paints the promises of God in the prophetic positioning and power of the Lord, radiantly displaying artwork from on high.

Humbly, Lynne gives thanks to her heavenly Father above for the privilege of co-creating with Him on this incredible journey with her art.

CONNECT WITH LYNNE HERE:

www.lynnehudson.com

lynne@lynnehudson.com

Gripped by the Gospel of His presence

The Lord Jesus welcomes us — rich, poor, unknown, famous, proud, humble, scared, brave, dirty, and clean — to each and all, the gospel of grace awaits. His gospel of grandeur, delight and wonder is a tender gift placed in each of our hands. Will it be opened? Will we receive a free gift from the land of His heavenly abode? Will we open the weight of His sacrificial love? Will we humbly receive something we can never earn? May you meet Jesus, and your Father in Heaven as you feel His lavished love; the very presence of God with us. Jesus Christ did what we can not physically do — die on the cross and atone for the entirety of sin for all of humanity. He hung there on the cross of crucifixion for you and for me, not because we are good and grand, but because His infinite love is just that and much more — adorned by grace and fashioned from love. Our Father in Heaven deemed Christ's sacrifice for our wrongdoings as the only solution to the injustice of our very sin. You and I. We are broken, we are hurting, and we are sinners. We are desperate for God to intervene in our lives and save us from our selfishness, our pain and our own earthly gain. Come as you are. Come with me, come yonder into the courts of His presence, into lands of His lavished love; where there is no judgment or fear, where the breath of God is really near! Come in, you are welcome, you and yours, to sit down at His table and bask in His great love for you. No longer rejected, but eternally accepted. Now you may ask, what can I do to be saved? It's as simple and as grandiose as this! Call upon His name, the name of Jesus. His holy blood of forgiveness awaits you with unrelenting grace. The displays of His providential wells of love never run out! You can be free, and run into an explosion of grace, awe and wonder. The invitation has been passed and now it is yours to receive!

ROMANS 10:13 (NIV)
FOR "EVERYONE WHO CALLS ON THE NAME OF THE LORD WILL BE SAVED."

A Prayer to Pray

I am a sinner. I have sinned against a perfect holy God, and my sins have hurt myself and others. Jesus, I want to be free! I want to know You. I want to hear Your voice. Would You forgive me for my sins, and take away the heavy burden of shame and guilt from my shoulders? Would salvation in You give me rest, eternally and here in Your presence on Earth? I believe in You. I trust that You died for my sins — past, present and future. I'm ready to soar with You into lands of lavished love.

I am Yours and You are mine, thank You that I can now shine as a star in the sky and the twinkle in Your eye. You are my love, sent from Heaven above. I now receive Your holy dove!

Crowned

Come one come all, children of the sin-filled fall.
Incline your hearts and bend your ears.
Can you sense My comforting presence is near?
I can come as a whisper, or a loud brilliant thunder.
I promise you, with Me you'll never ever plunder.
I am Your God, your King to save, hiding you from a life of tempestuous waves!
I have chosen you and your faith to grow.
I have crowned you, My child, with an everlasting glow.
You are loved, little one of Mine; let the heavens open and let my glory shine!
You are dearly precious to Me as My love impedes,
desiring to grow in you faith-bloomed seeds.
You are mine and I am yours, more than this world could ever war.
I am mighty in strength, deed, and power, and I promise you I will
provide comfort in your darkest hour.
Come to me, I am the King. I will show you wonders and glorious things!
I am good, loving and kind, sure to keep your every desire in mind.
We were made for one another; a deep intimate relationship,
so come to My table of honor and take a sip!
I died for you and desire to take your sin, and in exchange
give you eternal life, so you can win!
Reach high to the heavens with your arms open wide.
I promise I will pour My great love inside!
Receive, receive My love, My dearest little one, and I will guide you as you come!
In order to show you My love forever more, it is your very sin that I sacrificially bore.
YOU were worth it, little child of great grace,
I invite you to enter into realms of My holy place.
Where My little girl's praises rise up in great glory,
reaching high and declaring Christ's love as her ultimate story.

Prophetic Power

You are on a path meandering toward Heaven. As you reach the grass line, step over into Heaven's realm. The lollipop trees represent your childlike faith; your youthful imagination, just like balloons, expressing freedom and joy. Reach high for the stars, let your dreams fly on the clouds. The flowers are not connected to the earth, they are dancing. There is a freedom again — new life, budding excitement, new growth.

- Lynne Hudson

Prospering Promise

Give thanks to the Lord, for He is good. His love endures forever.

PSALM 39:1 (NIV)

Prayer

Grow in me a new song of victory, empowered by childlike faith and trust in You. Allow my life to be permeated with freedom; forever praising You as the great Son of glory. Bind up my mind with thoughts that praise You with clouds of great heavenly glory. Shine upon me, my Lord, as the beacon of my life. Illuminate my path with Your holy understanding. Triumphant communion with You is what I long for!

His Nature

Singing skies belt out praises to our one
true God who created Heaven and earth!

Charismatic clouds dance in joy at the Lord's name,
as they move to and fro in His amazing painting of Glory!

Motivating moon shines boldly to light up darkness and
remind us of His ever-glowing presence with us in every season.

Surging sun blinds us with His glory and brings warmth to our bodies
and hearts, enveloping us in the radiant power of His love.

Twirling trees trust in God's power to grow them, sustain them, and feed
them; singing songs of praise that soar into the wind with gladness.

A garden of His goodness — giving us life, hope, joy, and peace abundantly;
growing our roots deep into the nourishment of His presence and Word!

Raging raindrops remind us of God's faithful promise to take care of His
world and bring us manna from His heavenly abode.

Active animals prowl, live wildly, and navigate the earth
to show us His creative, mighty hand.

A river of redemption rages, remaining active
and providing abundance to a thirsty land.

Creation sings, our souls yearn, awaiting our eternal
place in Heaven, set aside for our lives for all of eternity!

His everlasting love covers the land and serves as
an inheritance and promise to all who would trust in HIM.

A land of grace, enthralled in His goodness, awaits
His chosen ones; capturing our hearts and minds with a haven
of His comforting love.

Prophetic Power

Raging raindrops remind us of God's promises (the rain on the right). This rain coming down from the sky partners with the rainbow, God's promises. These promises flood our lives as they meander through every curve of our journey with the Lord. The owl represents the wisdom of the Lord always keeping watch over us through our life's story. The swirling clouds look like a wave, a refreshing wave of the living waters. The butterfly represents new beginnings as we ponder the beauty of God's nature that surrounds us daily.

- Lynne Hudson

Prospering Promise

Let the heavens rejoice, let the earth be glad; let the sea resound, and all that is in it. Let the fields be jubilant, and everything in them, let all the trees of the forest sing for joy.

PSALM 96:11-12 (NIV)

Prayer

Father God, immerse me in Your living waters. Use every raindrop in my life as power-filled promises of Your providential plans. Allow my heart to experience Your creation, and my mind to be fixated on Your goodness through the radiant colors of Your faithful love. Let Your promises, signified in the rainbow, fill my life with comforting truth. Give me Your wisdom all the days of my life and allow my heart to be wholly communing with the presence of Your Holy Spirit.

Paradigms of Praise

Little girl, little boy, surrender your heart.

God made you to worship from the very start!

Worship, worship, throw up your hands, give Him
a shout and dance in the sands!

Little girl, little girl, give Him a twirl.

Worshipthe King, and let Him hear you sing.

Little boy, little boy, be filled with His joy.

Lavished in wonder, and filled with His Holy thunder.

Little girl, little boy, it's now time to soar!

To worship, to shout, and dance on the floor,
is an expectation to be filled with more!

Move, move little one!

Give Him a groove, and you will be sure to
make His loving heart move.

Sing, sing, little one!

The sound of your voice reaches the bright shining sun.

Lift up a melody and belt out a tune!

He loves you even more than His great beaming moon!

Praise, praise, let your voice rise.

Our awesome God wants to give you a surprise.

Reach, reach, reach little love.

His power you are grasping from Heaven above;
immersed in His presence, encircled by His holy dove.

Prophetic Power

Dancing in the sands with gay abandon, drumming to the beat of glorious praise; dancing and twirling while encircled in His love and grounded to His pure heart, which is the love heart in the sand.

The sound of the children's voices and music of praise reaches the heavens through the innocence of love hearts. What goes up with praise comes down with God's promises, which are represented by the rainbow colored love hearts. Children are trusting God's promises with their childlike faith. God's beauty of nature is nestled in the sands, showing us His all-encompassing masterpiece that He has created for us to enjoy.

- Lynne Hudson

Prospering Promise

Let Israel rejoice in their Maker; let the people of Zion be glad in their King. Let them praise His name with dancing and make music to Him with timbrel and harp. For the Lord takes delight in his people; He crowns the humble with victory. Let His faithful people rejoice in this honor and sing for joy on their beds.

PSALM 149:3-5 (NIV)

Prayer

Lord Jesus, bestow upon us worship-filled hearts rejoicing in Your perfect presence. Let our voices proclaim Your greatness, while our hands bless Your name and glorious fame. Let us spread Your love through the mouthpiece of our hearts, bringing Your will down to earth as it is in Heaven. May our praises rise up to Heaven to worship our King.

His Lavished Love

Beaming sun, rising on the horizon of the bay.

Dashing deer scatter at the sound of the morning.

The hum of the bees awake to the aroma of the sweet flowers.

Sun rays surge the morning with God's tender care awakening the dawn.

Light glimmers through the trees, canvassing canopies
of shade and glistening about.

Soothing, singing songs rise up to God through each breath
of the birds, tweeting His truths.

The favor of the Lord designated this day to reveal His gestures of great grace.

The gracious goodness of our of God feeds the birds and clothes
His children with His plentiful provisions.

His heart's patter paints colorful canvases upon the
earth with revelatory blues, oranges, and red hues.

Revealing His brilliant display and array of His royal wonder,

His arrangements of gushing glory splash us with reigning lavished love.

His paramount pleasure in His children is unceasingly expressed
through the beauty all around us.

The Lord's majestic, reflected image, painted throughout the depths of the earth,
invites us to enter into His presence, with a song of worship and adoration
bellowing into the heavenlies.

Prophetic Power

God's faithful love and blessings are always pouring out to us from every sunrise. His liquid love of richness meanders into our daily lives full of hidden treasures. Look for these treasures as you go throughout your day. Admire His handiwork of the exquisite creations of nature. What is around you? Enjoy the melodies of the birdsong as their notes twirl forever up to the heavens, bringing alive the joy in our day. The purple royalty (the main bird) is our righteousness in knowing that we are truly loved and cherished by Him.

- Lynne Hudson

Prospering Promise

For great is Your love, higher than the heavens;
Your faithfulness reaches to the skies.
Be exalted, O God, above the heavens;
Let Your glory be over all the earth.

PSALM 108:4-5 (NIV)

Prayer

Father God, Your spontaneous, yet pointed love brings us, as Your children, great joy. Would You teach us Your truths of old through the canvas of nature? Would You tell us of Your great faithfulness through the rising of the sun, and the beaming colors of the flowers? Wrap us in Your encompassing presence through experiencing Your light through creation. Hold us as we revel and treasure the dismays and awes of our surroundings. Thank You, Father God for being faithful to love us unceasingly. Bless my heart as I admire Your handiwork.

Cherished Children

Laughter of children, dazzling the world with great joy.

A bubbling of wonder rising up in each girl and boy.

Giggles, living deep, arising when learning flows,

Reveling and treasuring new concepts, from their heads to their toes.

Their smiles grow in their parents, a rich sense of peace,

A true reminder that God's little ones are just on lease.

They are His, His making, every precious one.

Meaning more to Him than the radiance of the sun.

Their joy was created by the might of His hands.

Designed in great wonder to prosper the lands.

His children are far more precious than any rare jewel.

Intended to reject every boastful word of the folly-filled fool.

His children's laughter rises right up to the haven of His heart.

Marked for glory and greatness from their wondrous start.

Giggles and joys find flight at the displays of His love.

All part of mercy-filled miracles from Heaven above.

Prophetic Power

Pull down the joy from the Lord. The joy is cascading down like celebration ribbons and confetti, dancing to the movement of the children's laughter. Feel the love surround you like a bubbling up of love balloons. Every color is a testament to His ferocious love for you. You are a reflection of His shining jewel qualities. You are a precious part of Him. Know this as you grab hold of His majestic love and shining-bright fatherly brilliance.

- Lynne Hudson

Prospering Promise

The Spirit you received does not make you slaves, so that you live in fear again; rather, the Spirit you received brought about your adoption to sonship. And by Him we cry, "Abba, Father."

ROMANS 8:15 (NIV)

Prayer

Father God, we are asking for ribbons of healing to flow onto the earth as it is in Heaven, touching each of Your children with a miracle. May every child reading this who is physically ill be healed by mercy ribbons of Your woven love. We ask that joy would rise from the compassionate care that You've rained down. We ask for renewed joy to flow from the body of believers onto all the earth. We are praying and asking for surpassing hope to shower Your Church, giving us Your mighty strength to prevail against our enemies.

Glory Galaxies

Come away with me into the mysteries of space —

a favorite, treasured, created place.

Journey off to the elevated moon —

all along, singing a heavenly tune.

Declare the vastness of His mighty power —

a display of glory during this very hour.

Galaxies and stars beyond man's wisdom —

all bound up in a glorious prism.

Revel in the land that is not lost —

that God redeemed when He sent His son with great cost.

A telling tale of the miracles beyond,

a display of His great love, so very fond.

Enjoy cataclysmic grace, dancing with the stars —

all shooting with excellence all the way to Mars.

Capture in a photo the land beyond our reach —

a perfect display of His presence, a platform to teach.

Enjoy revelations of soaring science and space sights —

get ready to launch with God on these bold, unfathomable flights.

Soaring beyond, on His wings of great power —

treasuring the fiery creations resting above any tower.

Illuminate with zeal the mysteries of space —

all throughout the globe, an incredibly unique place.

Prophetic Power

You are dressed in the royalty of purple as you have the privilege of reveling in God's heavenly creation. Rest in His vastness of goodness. Let the angels watch over you as you catch the stars that hold your destiny. Awaiting is the path of joy and excitement for what is to come, little one.

- Lynne Hudson

Prospering Promise

Lord, our Lord, how majestic is your name in all the earth! You have set your glory in the heavens. Through the praise of children and infants you have established a stronghold against your enemies, to silence the foe and the avenger. When I consider Your heavens, the work of Your fingers, the moon and the stars, which you have set in place, what is mankind that You are mindful of them, human beings that You care for them? You have made them a little lower than the angels and crowned them with glory and honor.

PSALM 8:1-5 (NIV)

Prayer

Jesus, we ask that You would fly us to the heavenlies with You, soaring on new heights into lands conquered by and through Your Holy Spirit. Would You teach us the hidden mysteries of the galaxies and impart to us radical faith-built wisdom from Your Holy Spirit. Would You allow us Heaven glimpses, so we can teach and love with an urgent, fiery faith. Would You allow us to celebrate with the angels when one sinner repents. Give us holy paths of victories, anointed in Your truth.

Brimming Beauty

Brimming beauty — bravery within.
Brimming beauty — forgiven from sin.
Brimming beauty — filled with His grace.
Brimming beauty — running the race.
Brimming beauty — where love abounds.
Brimming beauty — listening to His sounds.
Brimming beauty — beneath her skin.
Brimming beauty — victories within.
Brimming beauty — basking in His power.
Brimming beauty — ministering in this hour.
Brimming beauty — hearing His holy call.
Brimming beauty — glory despite the fall.
Brimming beauty — clothed in splendor.
Brimming beauty — a heart that is tender.
Brimming beauty — abiding in the One.
Brimming beauty — following His Son.
Brimming beauty — burning with fire.
Brimming beauty — raised out of mire.
Brimming beauty — His chosen love.
Brimming beauty — kept in His Dove.

Prophetic Power

As you praise God and surrender to Him, the Holy Spirit's breath hovers. The drops of His grace drip down from the heavens and are attached to the rivers flowing from His realm. The path meanders and His love becomes one with us. Let the budding new life (roses) be birthed inside and fill your little bodies. The ruffles are His delicate weaving that evolves into a blue/green sea of His comforting word — there is the fire of courage needed for the journey. It is a breaking of dawn where God's glory ministers to His precious ones.

- Lynne Hudson

Prospering Promise

…and provide for those who grieve in Zion— to bestow on them a crown of beauty instead of ashes, the oil of joy instead of mourning, and a garment of praise instead of a spirit of despair. They will be called oaks of righteousness, a planting of the Lord for the display of his splendor.

ISAIAH 61:3 (NIV)

Prayer

Lord Jesus, give us freedom where we are shackled. Breathe upon us the presence of Your Holy Spirit. Let Your dove be upon us as we hunger and thirst for Your presence. Allow Your richness to wash over us with infinite graces surrounding us. Let the heavens be opened, as we receive an outpouring of Your mercy — tasting and seeing that the Lord is good. May Your prominent peace-filled love rest in our hearts and may we be crowned with Your fashioned presence, promising us eternal life.

Fearless Followers

Children, children — do you know?

God made you precious and He loves you so.

Children, children — can you hear?

God's word is speaking and He's always near.

Children, children — persevere!

And let His ever-loving presence cast off all fear.

Children, children — you must overcome.

Stand firm against the enemy and remember where you're from.

Children, children — feast on His word.

Fill your heart with goodness, and soar high as a bird.

Children, children — revere and fear.

Long to enter His courts with joy and be ready to hear.

Children, children — be filled with His grace.

Our repentance brings Him a radiant smile on His face.

Children, children — feel His love overflow.

Working within you, His heavenly light to show.

Children, children — taste and see.

Enjoy the promises of His care as you soar and fly free.

Prophetic Power

Joy! Joy! As you hear God's word (blue), surrender to His lullaby and drench yourself in it, saturating in His promises. Let His word be like a waterfall, quenching your curiosity, quenching your desire to hear His voice. Let it permeate around you and drink it in. His glory is pouring down, turning into joyful ribbons, and partnering with the ribbons of your path. Fly like this bird on the road that He has chosen for you; the path is full of joy and unexpected delights. His living water is a continual stream of colors of new life, new beginnings, His glory and courage. You are like the little birds that drink from His Word. Be sure to remember to step out and take flight to fulfill your destiny.

- Lynne Hudson

Prospering Promise

Blessed are those who fear the Lord, who find great delight in His commands. Their children will be mighty in the land; the generation of the upright will be blessed. Wealth and riches are in their houses, and their righteousness endures forever. Even in darkness light dawns for the upright, for those who are gracious and compassionate and righteous. Good will come to those who are generous and lend freely, who conduct their affairs with justice. Surely the righteous will never be shaken; they will be remembered forever. They will have no fear of bad news; their hearts are steadfast, trusting in the Lord.

PSALM 112:1-7 (NIV)

Prayer

Father God, let us bask in Your freedom of grace, tasting Your truth with a believing heart. Let us fly as free as a bird into our destiny, soaring on the wings of Your gospel. Let Your love saturate us.

Revive Revive

Revive, revive

Awaken God's glorious love inside.

Return, return

Make my heart wildly burn.

Reveal, reveal

Your joy inside makes me squeal.

Speak, speak

Transform my heart and make me meek.

Revere, revere

Show me Your love by taking away every fear.

Toil, toil

Filled with strength, scattering seeds on soil.

Fight, fight

Using Your Word to scatter my enemies with Your might.

Shine, shine

Clinging to Your promises, Your grace is mine.

Fill, fill

Bringing me to a glory-filled, freedom hill.

Hear, hear

Listening to Your voice, and drawing joyfully near.

Shout, shout

Declaring Your name, chasing out looming doubt.

Prophetic Power

The warmth of His love in your heart is like a glorious sun showering down upon our world. We use His strength to fight our battle together, to sow the seeds in His glorious garden. The seeds are nurtured to produce warrior disciples in His land (sunflowers mean disciples). The different colored sunflowers are the "called" nations. You use your spade to turn new ground, to make way for new seasons with God. Dig deeper to apply the Word and see the fruit of your labor with Him. The butterflies represent new life, new creations in God, twirling effortlessly in His love.

- Lynne Hudson

Prospering Promise

You, Lord, keep my lamp burning; my God turns my darkness into light. With your help I can advance against a troop with my God I can scale a wall. As for God, His way is perfect: The Lord's word is flawless; He shields all who take refuge in him. For who is God besides the Lord? And who is the Rock except our God? It is God who arms me with strength and keeps my way secure. He makes my feet like the feet of a deer; He causes me to stand on the heights. He trains my hands for battle; my arms can bend a bow of bronze.

PSALM 18:28-34 (NIV)

Prayer

Let the beaming rays of Your Son's love reach me, giving me strength to face every trial and battle here on earth. Cultivate in my heart a grace garden, fully immersed in the blood of Jesus and the cross. Let my heart adore You, fixing my eyes on the Son continually. Give us joy in our eternal garden of communion. Jesus, be my best friend. Let salvation grow in me richly, magnifying Your grace and love.

Held

You paid my price once and for all,
by ransoming my life from the very great Fall.

My debt was paid when Your love made a way.

Victory has spoken and is here to stay.

Your thoughts for me outnumber the sparkling sand.

Promising Your presence to go forth in this land.

Your glorious love made a valiant way.

To harbor Your Spirit in my heart to stay.

Your greatness in power is too much to hold.

That is why You equip the Church to carry the load.

Your wisdom gives Your children a great mighty thunder.

Rescuing the lost from their desperate plunder.

Your miracles create a wondrous display.

Giving courage to Your people every single day.

Your power goes forth in love and will not stop.

Radiant, glory streams from Heaven's top.

Those who believe will be filled to the brim.

Worshiping His triumphant light that will never dim.

Faith travels down in rivers of delight.

Those that take hold will be filled with great might.

Rescuing redemption displaying great peace,
promised new life that will never cease.

Prophetic Power

Go deep, go to your quiet place and linger on the sacrifice Jesus made for us. We live out His promises through His almighty love. His truths are real. Feel them, they are tangible. They are all around us. Dip your toes in and feel His love. We are one with Jesus, and we reflect His image. The grass and the trees sway with delight to His voice. Listen, do you hear Him? Feel His all encompassing love, you are being held by your heavenly Father.

- Lynne Hudson

Prospering Promise

Yet to all who did receive him, to those who believed in His name,
He gave the right to become children of God.

JOHN 1:12 (NIV)

Prayer

Father God, allow these rainbows of Your love-filled promises to envelop me. Give me deep comfort, resting in the truth that Your sacrifice on the cross for my sin was enough to bring me into the presence of our Father. Give me trust as I surrender all to You my Lord. Allow the cross of Christ to be made the center of my life, that I may receive the gift of Your living water. Let me commune with You in and through the beauty of Your creation. Let every tree dance in praise. Let every duck quack Your glory, let every bird sing of Your mercy. Let joy fill me as I spend time with You. Fill my life with rivers of faith, permeating all that I am with Your Holy Spirit.

Deep Calls to Deep

Elegantly woven by God's mighty hand, you,
little daughter were created to prosper His great land.

Chosen before time, set apart by His love, your tender
heavenly Father pursues you from Heaven above.

Come into His bountiful garden, come enter into His grace.

Stand still and feel the joy dancing through the smile on His face.

His love for you is endless, He will never let you down.

He's there to wipe your tears and comfort your saddened frown.

Come look a little yonder, breathe in His calming air.

His presence is always with you to hold your every care.

Hold His hand and walk as you ponder His precious word,
let Him tend to your heart as you soar freely as a bird.

Look at all the great sights, the beauty all around, and imagine
that you are greater to Him than every lovely sound.

Your beauty is enchanting, your heart is more precious than gold.

He forever loves to pursue you and you are His to hold.

Enter into His presence, feel the warmth of His heart.

Feel His glory all around you, and remember that He
loved you right from the very start.

Prophetic Power

Daughter of the Most High, you are His masterpiece created by His palette. You only have to reach out and receive from Him. Feel the joy bouncing off His creations. Look deeply and see His endless love for you. It surrounds you, engulfs you. Every day He is raining down His liquid love of blessings to encourage and refresh you. Drink it in. The dew drops are kisses from Heaven. God's beauty is reflected in all His creations. His glory is all around.

- Lynne Hudson

Prospering Promise

The Lord will guide you always; He will satisfy your needs in a sun-scorched land and will strengthen your frame. You will be like a well-watered garden, like a spring whose waters never fail.

ISAIAH 58:11 (NIV)

Prayer

Father God, give me a continual supply of new life, blossoming from Your heart to mine. Allow my eyes to follow the Son, for all the God-growth in my life. Be my sustaining grace, in my sin and in my service to You. Allow my heart to surrender to the warmth of Your grace and richness of Your mercy. Let not one of Your Holy Spirit seeds of saving grace be wasted in my life. Jesus, teach me what it means to surrender trying to be perfect, humbly positioned in a resting stature before You, drinking from Your well of grace when I sin. Let me see that my sin is to bring me to Your cross of eternal life, ushering me always into Your presence. Give me a deep need of Your guidance, power and strength. Jesus, I confess I can't do this without Your Spirit. Let me follow You like the sunflowers follow the sun. You will supply all that I need.

Come Away

Soar Free

With your heavenly Father's glee.

Come away

Into fields of creative play.

Sing a song

To the praise of Jesus all day long.

Explore with Him

And you'll feel joy right up to the brim.

Bask in His love

As He sings over you from abodes above.

Work and toil

Feel the anointing power of His holy oil.

And when you rise

Look to God with thankful eyes.

Always know

The Lord God is with you wherever you shall go.

It is His love from above

That He rests on you like a gentle dove.

So take comfort, my friend

The everlasting love of the Lord will never end.

Prophetic Power

Use your pure, joyful, innocent imagination and play with your loving Jesus. Fly high to the heavens, fly with glee and praise with your song. You are blessed with His love songs for you, weaving their melody upon your path. His oil is a richness of gold pouring out to drench your appetite to know Him, to feel His love. The heavens of His love are forevermore.

- Lynne Hudson

Prospering Promise

I will sing of the Lord's great love forever; with my mouth I will make Your faithfulness known through all generations. I will declare that your love stands firm forever, that You have established your faithfulness in heaven itself.

PSALM 89:1-2 (NIV)

Prayer

My Lord, bring me into the heights of Your heavenly courts, soaring free. The Son has set me free! Let me be filled with Holy Spirit-filled freedom, as I learn who You are. May the grace and love of Your presence fill me with power and strength to soar with You. Allow all the enemy's schemes in my life to be put to shame, as I rise above what the adversary intended for harm. Your presence allows me to soar above the clouds, keeping me safe all the days of my life. Let me look down upon my enemies, as I fly free into my destiny with King Jesus. As I fly, let me worship You, creating a heavenly song, booming in unison with the choir of angels.

Under His Pinions

A storm is surging little one

Yet He holds you, strengthens you and loves you a ton.

His tender care upon you, as the lightning gives a flash

No storm will make your mighty, powerful protector dash.

As the turbulent waves rise high

Rest assured they will never reach the sky.

You can be kept in the sweetness of His song

Declaring that God is with you all the day long.

The plenty of the Lord continues to provide

Offering you His presence so you can freely abide.

Have no fear of the assailing danger

For that is why the Savior came for you in a meager manger.

Give Him your every tear, fear and pain

Trust Him completely as He teaches you through the rain.

A tender Father who loves to feed you care

Even when the roaring storm continues to boisterously blare.

Take heart, dearly beloved child

The suffering you face is only quite mild.

The King of all Kings has protected your place

Under the pinions of His wildest grace.

Take courage, my sweet friend

Your tender heart indeed, does He wholly mend.

Prophetic Power

He has you in the storm. His feathers are your sail to guide you through the turbulent waters of life. The boat is your security, symbolic of being held by your heavenly Father, anchored in His love. The dove is always with you, your comforter, teacher and guidance. God's love shines above you; it always breaks up a storm and brings calm waters. Although the lightning might strike, God's love keeps it at bay.

- Lynne Hudson

Prospering Promise

When you pass through the waters, I will be with you; and when you pass through the rivers, they will not sweep over you.

ISAIAH 43:2 (NIV)

Prayer

Father God, turn my trials and sorrows into joy. As I go through spiritual warfare and surging storms of life, show me the evidence of Your presence. Bring peace to my heart as I patiently endure the suffering of this lifetime. Transform, mold and shape me into Jesus' image. Teach me the truths of Your Word, breathing into me the peace and comfort of Your presence. You are with me in the storm. Reassure my heart and enlighten my mind with Your Holy Word. Increase my faith and trust in You, oh Risen One.

Oceans of Delight

Feel the gentle touch of the soft warm breeze.

Embrace the pure water rushing to your knees.

Smell the salty sweet air
and experience God's love there.

Feel the sun kissing your cheeks
and revel in the pelicans' large beaks.

Feel the warmth of the golden smooth sand.

Enjoy sights of the vast ocean that covers the land.

Frolic boldy in the tide of the roaring wave.

Be planted firmly in the God who saves.

Swim, explore and dive deep down,

remembering that your God gives you a crown.

Rejoice as you enter into the presence of His rest

and remember that Jesus Christ truly loves you best.

Enjoy blessings of this heavenly profound place
as joys by the sea bring a warm smile to your face.

Thank the one who made it all
and listen to His Holy Spirit's comforting call.

Prophetic Power

God's love is a mosaic of swirling colors as you go deeper into His presence. The joy of His wonders surround you as you bask in the glory of His brand new day. His gentle surprises that you find, are a treasure chest of golden opportunities as you discover His playful creations. Explore and discover!

- Lynne Hudson

Prospering Promise

You answer us with awesome and righteous deeds, God our Savior, the hope of all the ends of the earth and of the farthest seas, who formed the mountains by Your power, having armed Yourself with strength, who stilled the roaring of the seas, the roaring of their waves, and the turmoil of the nations. The whole earth is filled with awe at Your wonders; where morning dawns, where evening fades, You call forth songs of joy. You care for the land and water it; You enrich it abundantly.

PSALM 65: 5-9 (NIV)

Prayer

Abba Father, take me to Heaven's abode, to a quiet place in the glory of Your presence. Let me interact in great delight with the wonder of Your creations, as I talk to You about the joys and beauty of this world. Let me freely experience the goodness of God through the outpouring of Your mercy on all of Your creation. May songs of glory well up in my heart, treasuring You above all else as I revel at Your handiwork. May love shine and grow wildly in my heart, echoing praises and glory unto Your name. May words and adorations flow from my mind as I ponder what You have made and how much You love me. Expand to me the heavenlies, and access to Your Spirit.

Portions of Grace

There's a grace portion waiting for you.

Portions of grace ready to give you a feast of forgiveness.

Portions of grace ready to adorn your laugh with the King's love.

Portions of grace carrying you to exhilarating measures and heights.

Portions of grace ushering you into His tangible peace-filled presence.

Portions of grace delegated to you from the Father's faithful generosity.

Portions of grace raining down in Sonlight rays of His prominent delight.

Portions of grace ready to inspire the work of your hands.

Portions of grace leading to hidden discoveries of His manifold wisdom.

Portions of grace catching you when you crumble, stumble and fall.

Portions of grace equipping you to carry His great name.

Portions of grace pouring the fruit of the Spirit into your heart.

Portions of grace birthing great victories in His children across the globe.

Portions of grace wrap around you from Heaven above.

Do you feel it, child of God?

Prophetic Power

Receive the gifts of grace God has for you. Be excited, just like a cozy Christmas morning, opening the grandest present of all from your heavenly Father. He has many gifts for you. Explore them, treasure them. They are there to nurture you. Ribbons mean gifts; You are grounded in His promises. Be comfortable in His wrap-around love.

- Lynne Hudson

Prospering Promise

For it is by grace you have been saved, through faith—and this is not from yourselves, it is the gift of God—not by works, so that no one can boast.

EPHESIANS 2: 8-9 (NIV)

Prayer

May Your grace be the food I feast on, and the gift I receive over and over as an expression of the outpouring of Your love and faithfulness. May the gift of my salvation, the blood You shed for me on the cross, be opened as I trust and put my faith in You. May miracles flow from Your holy throne, as I watch Your glory manifest here on earth. May the fruits of the Spirit — goodness, joy, peace, patience, kindness, faithfulness, generosity, self control, and love — be the marks of Your presence upon me. Fill me with pure joy, as I fully trust in You.

Mend Me

Mend me. Send me. To the lingering lost.

Mend me. Send me. No matter the cost.

Mend me. Send me. To lands far from reach.

Mend me. Send me. Bringing Your love to preach.

Mend me. Send me. With Your lavished love.

Mend me. Send me. With Your power from above.

Mend me. Send me. To heal the sick.

Mend me. Send me. To light the fire of their wick.

Mend me. Send me. To bind a broken heart.

Mend me. Send me. Revealing Jesus from the start.

Mend me. Send me. Fleeing evil and rising high.

Mend me. Send me. To bring mercy to every lost cry.

Mend me. Send me. To sound aloud Your protective roar.

Mend me. Send me. To help others fruitfully soar.

Mend me. Send me. To fight the good fight.

Mend me. Send me. Rescuing Your children in the dark of night.

Mend me. Send me. To bring good news to the poor.

Mend me. Send me. To proclaim who all this is really for!

Mend me. Send me. In the face of the evil snake.

Mend me. Send me. Seeing Your enemies run, hide and shake.

Mend me. Send me. To proclaim Your saving blood.

Mend me. Send me. To revive many with a Holy Spirit flood.

Prophetic Power

Because of your received healing, God has equipped you to transform lives, to step out and conquer new lands, new territories. You have on your Holy backpack, the Word of God. The fire of the Holy Spirit fills you. He is with you like a gentle dove on your shoulder.

As you heal, His promises are birthed from on high. His promises for you are like a flood, nourishing you as you travel along His path, His plan that He has for you. The squirrel is the "one" that we stop for along the way, to nourish and plant a seed of hope.

- Lynne Hudson

Prospering Promise

For You have been my hope, Sovereign Lord,
my confidence since my youth.

PSALM 71:5 (NIV)

Prayer

Jehovah-Jireh, You are the Lord our provider. You provide me with everything I need. I ask that I would embrace the journey You have laid out for me. Help me to see You, leaning on You as the staff of victory. Let me walk down rainbows of Your divinity, paths of peace, wearing a backpack of preparation. Allow all the tools of Your Word, the power of Your Holy Spirit, and the access to Your power, be held tightly to me as I travel into unchartered territories. Fill me with strength and awe-struck wonder as I revel at the intimacy of Your presence and the splendor and grandeur of Your beauty. I shall not fear, for You have redeemed me and called me by name.

An Oceans Roar Mimics God's Justice

Loud waves roll forth in the power of His name.

The wind drives the waves with a force to be reckoned with.

The boisterous might of His glory rolls in toward the shore.

Pelicans and seagulls dive and broach His Heaven-song.

Entities of God encircle His valiant creation.

No man can withstand the power of His might,

Nor can the eye fully comprehend the magnitude of His surging strength.

Clouds sit peacefully on shelves in the sky.

The sun's pressurized heat radiates warm delight.

Billowing revelations carry His care.

On wings of eagles soaring freedom speaks.

Stop, pause and wonder at the greatness of His majesty.

Worship our King in great reverence and trust!

Prophetic Power

Be in awe of the magnitude of His majesty and splendor. You are His mighty warrior, put your armor on and fight your battles. You have been given the inheritance of His power and grace. God is equipping you with His strength. Receive it, let it wash over you.

- Lynne Hudson

Prospering Promise

The Lord reigns, He is robed in majesty; the Lord is robed in majesty and armed with strength; indeed, the world is established, firm and secure. Your throne was established long ago; You are from all eternity. The seas have lifted up, Lord, the seas have lifted up their voice; the seas have lifted up their pounding waves. Mightier than the thunder of the great waters, mightier than the breakers of the sea—the Lord on high is mighty. Your statutes, Lord, stand firm; holiness adorns Your house for endless days.

PSALM 93 (NIV)

Prayer

Jesus, fill us with the power of Your blood and word, to tread on the serpents of falsity. Give us great courage to face any suffering with the justice of God at our right side and the peace of God at our left. Let us look to the majesty and dominion of our Lord. You are paving the way for free-soaring victories in every circumstance. We stand in Your might, as we hold our sword of the Spirit, the truth of God, and we shall not be moved. Soar within us the unrelenting love of the Spirit, bringing us into heavenly realms of authority.

Golden Glories

Turquoise truth
Purple promises
Blue breakthroughs
Pink pathways
Green gates
Yellow yearning
Red reigning
Brown bravery
Periwinkle peace
Orange orchestrating
White waterfalls
Jasper justice
Ivory invitations
Emerald enveloping
Primrose pursuits
Gray grace
Lilac love

Prophetic Power

Rest in your heavenly Father's presence as you lean back into your gates of praise. Know that He will rebuild your life and your situation. The truth is at your doorstep (turquoise stones). See the breakthroughs (the pockets of blue sky) from the Lord. Be grounded in His love, saturated in His goodness. Gaze on His miracles that surround you, the beauty of His hand; the hidden gems. Be refreshed by His waterfalls of living water, teardrops from Heaven. Let it meander along your path. You hold His precious heart.

- Lynne Hudson

Prospering Promise

Though the mountains be shaken and the hills be removed, yet my unfailing love for you will not be shaken nor my covenant of peace be removed," says the Lord, who has compassion on you. "Afflicted city, lashed by storms and not comforted, I will rebuild you with stones of turquoise, your foundations with lapis lazuli. I will make your battlements of rubies, your gates of sparkling jewels, and all your walls of precious stones. All your children will be taught by the Lord, and great will be their peace. In righteousness you will be established: Tyranny will be far from you; you will have nothing to fear. Terror will be far removed; it will not come near you. If anyone does attack you, it will not be my doing; whoever attacks you will surrender to you.

ISAIAH 54: 10-15 (NIV)

Prayer

Allow Your Kingdom's brilliance to cascade over our hearts, minds and souls. Allow us to stand at the door of Your presence and knock, seeking You all the days of our lives. Usher us into the unseen, the colorful infusions of Your love, oil, mercy and living presence. Crown Your people in triumph as we wholly surrender to Your will. Allow us to love You deeply and richly as every Kingdom color and profound beauty reaches the depths of our souls. Grow abounding wells of trust treasures in our hearts.

Wholly His

Wholly His, never apart from His infinite love and consuming pursuit.

Wholly His, a forever established covenant, a promise of faithfulness.

Wholly His, whenever I fear and wander in dark valleys of despair.

Wholly His, truly forgiven, my sins are cast into the bottomless depths of the sea.

Wholly His, a harbor of hope, satisfying my very being with enriching love.

Wholly His, calling me forward in ultimate surrender,
while flaming in me an unquenchable fire.

Wholly His, a protector avenging the enemy who encircles me with lies.

Wholly His, captivating encouragement propelling
me forward into lavished purpose.

Wholly His, shouldering my cares and delivering me from deadly pestilence.

Wholly His, an armor of light, carrying His torches of
truth into a land that is perishing.

Wholly His, His tangible provisions too incredible to
number, an endless array of mercy manna.

Wholly His, releasing, in me and through me, His power and
strength to take His gospel to the ends of the earth.

Wholly His, never separated, never without,
my sure foundation and Savior of my soul.

Prophetic Power

Shut out the darkness and revel in His light. Bathe in the warmth of His fire of love, which encompasses your very being. Feed from His burning goodness, as you are wrapped up in His love. He encircles you with His strength. When you glimpse into the heavens, pull back the curtain of darkness to reveal His promises. They are always there as a reminder of His faithfulness pouring down upon you. Let the color break through the clouds to minister to your body, soul and spirit.

- Lynne Hudson

Prospering Promise

But you are a chosen people, a royal priesthood, a holy nation, God's special possession, that you may declare the praises of him who called you out of darkness into his wonderful light.

1 PETER 2:9 (NIV)

Prayer

We are asking that Your Kingdom come here on earth as it is in Heaven. Burn ablaze in my heart. Allow us to forgive those who have sinned against us as You have graciously forgiven us of all our trespasses. Let the radiant warmth of Your Holy Spirit's fire ignite us with Your love. Burn up all of our sinned-filled dross, with havens of Your comfort and deep, needed rest. We drink Your living water, which refreshes our souls and reminds us of the warmth of Your care and love for us. Thank You, Father, for sending us into a broken world, so we can be a living hope. Burn brightly within us, brilliantly displaying the power of Christ at work within our lives. Allow us to carry Your very presence to the nations with the truth of the gospel — bringing salvation to the captive, the sinner, the lonely, the afflicted, and the hungry.

www.ingramcontent.com/pod-product-compliance
Lightning Source LLC
Chambersburg PA
CBHW042052050526
44107CB00109B/1116